A Heart- Squeeze
of
Beginnings and Endings

by

Jenna Plewes

First published 2026 by The Hedgehog Poetry Press

Published in the UK by
The Hedgehog Poetry Press
5, Coppack House
Churchill Avenue
Clevedon
BS21 6QW

www.hedgehogpress.co.uk

ISBN: 978-1-916830-62-2

Copyright © Jenna Plewes 2026

The right of Jenna Plewes to be identified as the author of this work has been asserted in accordance with the Copyright, Designs and Patents Act 1988.

All rights reserved. No part of this publication may be reproduced, stored in or introduced into a retrieval system, or transmitted in any form, or by any means (electronic, mechanical, photocopying, recording or otherwise) without prior written permissions of the publisher. Any person who does any unauthorised act in relation to this publication may be liable for criminal prosecution and civil claims for damages.

9 8 7 6 5 4 3 2 1

A CIP Catalogue record for this book is available from the British Library.

Contents

The Winter Calvary 5

Waiting for Snowmelt 6

Falling Snow 7

Thistles in Winter 8

Thaw 9

In the Kingdom of the Egg 10

The Lovesong of Toads 11

Washed 12

Nightshirt 13

Sand 14

Everything's in Flux 15

A Summer's Day 16

A Generosity of Beginnings 17

On the Cusp 18

Harvesting potatoes 19

On listening to Schindler's List by John Williams 20

THE WINTER CALVARY

Stark as carrion stretched on a boundary wire
a shrivelled figure hangs on a cross

wind slaps grey rags of snow in its face
they stick to ribcage, kneecaps, finger bones,
trail from the long thin feet.

The traveller kneels bareheaded
his woollen coat muzzled, quiet,

sleet lashes the soft skin of his neck
the sky is the colour of flesh.

a scene depicted on a wooden panel in St Hilary's Church, Ludgvan, Cornwall.

WAITING FOR SNOWMELT

He's out there
bent as a crooked finger

searching for something
under the surface of a dream

bony fingers splay like starfish
trapped behind glass
bubbles blink like lidless eyes in the muddy depths

trees creak in the wind
rags of dead leaves
skitter across the ice

cracks widen, black water grins,
he turns, raises his head,
lifts a hand.

FALLING SNOW

its silent insistence

mesmerizes

kitten-soft touches
melt
on skin
on hair

each breath's
a white wreath

flake
follows
flake

padding
brokenness

smoothing
inconsistences

shielding
each
sharp
stone

forgiving
the muddle
and rubble
of existence

each
bent branch
each
troubled life

transformed.

THISTLES IN WINTER

Green starfish, pincushion sharp
I see them everywhere
now that the sheep have gone
turf bitten to the quick

hundreds of them,
some big as dinner-plates,
some tiddly-wink small
bristly Catherine Wheels
their thin white roots
pinning them down

each one unique
intricately patterned
beaded with mist
a thread of sheep wool
caught on its barbs
a feather, a leaf

in summer they stood tall
their shaving-brush heads
ruffled by bees

when the purple flowers
browned and bristled
goldfinches gorged
and scattered their seeds

now on the grey-green slopes of the hill
they wait out the winter.

THAW

The grip of winter's fingers on your throat
the slap and bite of air on cheeks and chin
trees lovely in their bare simplicity
a tracery of branches, black on white

the slap and bite of air on cheeks and chin
a sun too weak to melt the fur of frost
a tracery of branches, black on white
a frozen world, padlocked without a key

a sun too weak to melt the fur of frost
hard nubs of hazel buds, a frill of aconites
a frozen world, padlocked without a key
waiting for warmth, the softening of spring

hard nubs of hazel buds, a frill of aconites
needles of green pushing through muddy ground
waiting for warmth, the softening of spring
catkins breathing pollen on the wind

needles of green pushing through muddy ground
blackthorn flowering like fallen stars
catkins breathing pollen on the wind
new-born lambs with quivering tassel tails

blackthorn flowering like fallen stars
the slip of winter's fingers from your throat
new-born lambs with quivering tassel tails
trees lovely in their innocence of green.

IN THE KINGDOM OF THE EGG

I dreamt myself into an egg
safe within milk-white walls
pinpricked with light

a speck, a chip of garnet
on a pillow of honeyed yolk
I floated in an inland sea

it was not enough

I bloated a rubbery body, lidded eyes
sprouted claws and beak
scribbled scrawny wings

gripped in a marble fist

I seethed in my cell
chipped and chiselled
broke through the dome

staggered into a world of
chickweed and thistles
cloudburst and sunshine

unshelled
        unsafe
                awake

THE LOVESONG OF TOADS

What is it wakes them
deep in the ground
a stirring in the soil
a quickening of something?

Shrivelled, fasting
they haul themselves out
with a ravening hunger,
an irresistible urge to mate

crossing lanes and carriageways
potholes, speed bumps, tarmac and gravel
on a Russian roulette of a journey

drawn back to their birthing place
they skid down muddy ditches
plop into ponds, streams, pools

a bubbling soup of toads, a rolling
ball of leathery, warty bodies
clasping, clambering, clinging

falling, separating into pairs
for a long holding

a sonorous love song, breath by slow
breath until a final letting go
a solitary return, leaving behind

beaded necklaces looping the reeds
swaying in the flow of the stream.

WASHED

Sunrise
        sparks every blade of grass
leaves
      drip diamonds

light polishes
              a pile of cyclamen shields

the sky's swept and mopped
                  bluer than blue

indoors smells of soot
                dust and dead flies

a day to

peel a haze of dirt
                from every window pane

squeegee the glass
           till a glitterball of sunshine

fills every room
              and the garden streams in.

NIGHTSHIRT

The baggy tee shirt's soft
                cool against my skin each night
                              reaches my knees, covers my wrists

I'm wrapped in mountains
                a rising sun on my breast
                              a blaze of golden eyes guarding me
I'm stitched into S o l u k h u m b u
                wearing nothing underneath
                              the scarlet and gold embroidery
it smells of dust
        of stepped paths
                        the singing flute of a sherpa boy at dusk

of bedrolls and canvas
            story-telling
                      and laughter under diamond studded skies

            now

the shirt's rolled in a drawer
with walking trousers,
socks and blister packs
an ancient tube of sunscreen
glucose sweets

the scent of sweat and happiness
long washed away

SAND

I see you,
        surf swirling round your ankles
                dwarfed by an eternity of beach

your small body powdered with sand
        mica glinting your bare feet
                sand and salt rasping your wet skin

        later

I find more sand on the kitchen floor, sweep up
        the slow grinding of millennia into grit

and smaller, infinitely small
                the indelible stain of microplastic

the sea smooths away your footprints
        wind ruffles the dunes
                gulls scream, unclean, unclean.

EVERYTHING'S IN FLUX

Wind rakes the shore
pummels seagrass and mallow
whips the beach into gusts of stinging sand

gulls surf a cloudless sky, waves
batter the rocks, hiss and retreat,
the sea's blue and white, bright
as a delft dish.

Beneath the surface, bladderwrack and
kelp sway in the current, rubbery lips
mouth my skin

a riptide stronger than I can resist,
takes me far beyond the headland
and when it slackens

I must find a new way back.

A SUMMER'S DAY

It is one of those slow days, when nothing
much happens, that drip like resin
trapping each tiny detail in amber

butterflies laze on the buddleia
bees drone in the lavender
thicken the air with endless tinnitus

in the park children play in a skin of water
a woman strolls with a kitten on a lead
it lunges at a pigeon, patters on beside her

leaves are a pointillist pattern, green on blue
a breeze shifts ripples of light, pollen dusts
the surface of the pond, the children's hair.

A GENEROSITY OF BEGINNINGS

Listen to them

a soft tap after tap
            into leaf litter
gulp after gulp
            into the pond
a rattle like hail
            on the roof of the shed

cupfuls of summer falling into autumn

each acorn,
    a shiny brown egg
           snug in its cup

 fuses
       bouncing
            rolling
                  splitting

trampled
        husked
                snuffed out

one seedling oak
            flickering into flame.

ON THE CUSP

We choose the corner of a small field
sheltered by high hedges
tucked away from the main road

where the hum of traffic veers
like a weathervane
a whisper of surf, then gone.

My daughter gurgles and burbles
in her buggy while we pick
blackberries, our conversation
drowsy as the drone of foraging bees.

When the ripple of sound turns
into a wail, I sit in a trample of grasses
among the bric-a-brac of berries and seeds
the honey scent of ivy flowers, musk of rot

while she nuzzles and pulls my nipples
glutting herself in the lingering heat
of the slow falling away of summer.

HARVESTING POTATOES

It's time – before the first hard frost

in the valley the woods are cobwebbed and grey
only the oak sheltering the house still blazes
against a slate sky.

I carry the old metal bucket, you the garden forks
their long handles braced against your shoulder.

I take my side of the bed, you the other – as we always do –
bending like windblown trees, we lever up the left-over
haulms, find shrivelled potato mothers, their babies still
on stringy umbilical cords, sift through the soil for the rest
wipe them clean, smooth and round as eggs, count the clutch

 a good year for earlies

the main crop will be heavy digging, a harvest
surly as winter; great weathered fists raised against
the long cold dark. Meaty, misshapen, scarred
they'll keep us fed.

ON LISTENING TO SCHINDLER'S LIST BY JOHN WILLIAMS

The melody rises
           wide-winged as a condor over the Andes

the last three notes
           climbing razored peaks of joy and pain

a lifetime in a wingbeat
           feathered memories streaming the air

tinsel of poplar leaves in sunshine
           the chuckle of foraging hens

grip of a toddler's fingers
           smell of a lover's skin

shiver of lake water
           prickle of nettle stings

a heart-squeeze of beginnings
           and endings

slipping away.